FINANCIAL FREEDOM ROADMAP

FINANCIAL FREEDOM ROADMAP

ELARA PHOENIX

CONTENTS

CHAPTER 1

Introduction

Digital transformation and the shift to investments through modern mutual funds, exchange-traded funds, holdings of securities, and other modern investment products are similarly transforming the wealth and investment management industry, shifting consumers towards fee-based investing and planning. This book is a must-read for anyone looking to achieve financial freedom and security. The very use of the term 'building' assumes a strategic approach that entails prevention, nurturing, and, yes, some heavy lifting. I convey techniques for both the novice and the sophisticated investor. For those who are new to investing or want an even deeper understanding of our markets, we can explore the basic philosophies of investing, developing a basic understanding of the various investment products and their characteristics.

Today, more people than ever are recognizing the vital importance of building financial security and well-being. Even without the challenges of the ongoing COVID-19 pandemic, the combination of medical costs, retirement and education objectives, and other unforeseen lifestyle changes create an unrealized sense of financial urgency. Most financial transactions in the U.S. are digitally managed today; indeed, a 2019 survey by Morning Consult found that nearly half of all Americans use only digital tools to manage their finances.

The ability to assess personal financial status, craft investing strategies, and develop acceptable risk levels is now largely performed with the help of digital tools.

CHAPTER 2

Understanding Financial Freedom

As stated in the first section, financial freedom is financial independence, so what money needs to do for you to help build your financial freedom and retirement funds? Being able to earn money will help you: Meeting your basic needs such as food, shelter, and clothing. While enjoying life through the time and flexibility brought by hobbies and passion. Contribute to things of personal meaning and fulfillment. As being there for participants, time, money or assistance. Create an emotional and physical health balance. Builder of your technological work, or company. If you find it hard to awaken with financial and life goals in the morning, saving money for any reason won't create value for you. In fact, I strongly advocate spending money mostly through the expenses to protect the past, especially the experiences. For example, dining with friends and family, seeing exciting shows, traveling and dancing are the wonderful experiences that fun and long-lasting memories are worth experiencing (enjoying) a lifetime.

What is financial freedom? Words and phrases often have multiple definitions, so what does financial freedom bring to mind for you? Here are a few definitions that I found: 1. Having savings for an emergency happens. 2. Living within your means. 3. Having a secure paycheck. 4. Having a secure investment. 5. Having a secure job. 6. Having many assets for income generation after loosening the daily chores. 7. Being rich. Although there are many different definitions and opinions about what financial freedom is, it is important to remember that financial freedom is a unique interpretation of individuals according to their financial conditions, age, family composition, status, preferences, goals, and properties.

CHAPTER 3

Setting Financial Goals

S tart Building Wealth! Gaining financial freedom is not about getting lazy and making unplanned changes. Instead, it's about making informed choices that result in both wealth and security for the planning in the future. Depending on your current financial standing and your objectives, explicit measures will be taken. Some of these include: increasing your retirement plan savings to a ball-park of 10-20% annually, reducing your monthly income to below 28% and other recurrent costs since you should balance between debt repayment, spending and saving, and holding checks. Make sure you have the right insurance, especially if you are not safe, and raise your resources to invest in major markets to provide you some security. Remember that their relationship is unique too. To set your retirement and financial freedom target dates, it's wise to be opti-mistic about your income, but reasonable about your product. Arrange to review every year to review and make any necessary changes as personal developments occur.

Set SMART goals: It is worth setting financial targets if you take a smart approach. This essentially outlines the different character-istics of the objectives you have set, namely: being specific, mea-surable, achievable, relevant, and timely. For instance, do not just hope that your net worth will increase. Instead, set a specific amount that could result in a sufficient level of financial independence for you, say $1,000,000. Not only is this goal relevant, but it's also measurable. To make this useful, give a targeted amount to reach each month or year. Making a goal assigned can help you initiate the changes you need to save and spend appropriately, and the final point outlined makes the expected growth or target date to deploy so that you start taking good measures from now.

After assessing your financial situation, you can then embark on setting financial goals. This is particularly crucial since it can define financial freedom's expansive concrete steps. Without goals, a financial freedom plan may become sidelined by daily outgoings and setbacks, never making real progress. Something as minimal as using a rich life card that visually lists your financial goals increases the power of their optics to make them closer to reality. You can list your goals under six categories: financial independence, family, work, community, personal lives, and travel. For each financial-bound ambition, you should also provide a numeric target and the current status towards realizing the end result. Make these ambitious but realistic at the same time by setting an estimated fulfillment date and the next three targets. Most importantly, reassess your circumstances and make the necessary steps to ensure fluid adjustments towards the different financial goals.

CHAPTER 4

Creating a Budget

To make this work, you should concentrate on getting low or fixed expenses for most of the monthly budget items. Wherever you can do this, an emergency is a gift to you, freeing up money without blowing the rest of the universal budget. The monthly budget is paramount and only used for the month. The signatures on the original universal budget must have anticipated (matched), increased, or decreased money from the money actualized. As noted, this is a transfer to bring the budget to zero. The universal budget requires that the family spends money necessary to obtain a zero balance at the end of the day it is completed. This wired budget will still increase as the owner's control of his/her wealth does the same. Don't worry, the first family budget is usually the most difficult one to balance.

Your monthly budget is an estimate of how you plan to spend your money for the coming weeks. It uses past months' expenses as a basis for what you will need for this month. The budget is the starting place for everyone. That's where you gain control of your financial life. It solves the 24-hour money problem for the month. It is not a last-minute money problem, as it should be. This really works, so let's get the budget started. This is your first budget, to be revised in the future as you gain some control of your finances. If this is your first universal budget, it is better to err on the side of higher expenses. Sometimes, the expenses are more than the money, but in time and after working with the wealth-building steps, this will become your typical situation.

CHAPTER 5

Saving and Investing

There is another way to look at savings—by setting yourself regular personal goals in life. Generally, goals that require saving and accumulating money; that is: investment. And without this often stressful process, there will be no accumulated amount, only day to day expenses that will follow the small great desires. Time to talk about investing, then? Not sure if we are ready to name it yet... And 'investment'—isn't it considered to be a sacred word, a real mystery, and is it known to a few professional initiates with high-ranking qualifications? More and more young people, who are not in contemplation of old age, show a growing interest in the investment world in order to become survivors in the brutal and ruthless 'jungle' of currencies, the stock exchange, the market of capital and the real estate market. There is a mistaken conviction that only through investing, currency and the stock exchange can the practical end be achieved in a possible and unexpected start, which only wealthy people can achieve. SMERS: "Save-Moj-Denaro-Every-Mengia- Tied! Be merciful and committed only to do, and so also the young people around you, and that investing is an ally for the goal reached! The main idea is, Do what you can with what you have—today. It is necessary to define the term 'investment'. So let's start from here.

Saving is virtually the only habit that sets the foundation for financial freedom that everyone agrees on. But as almost no one actually does it the way that makes it the most powerful. What does 'saving' really mean in consumer societies? We put a certain amount of money aside to enjoy it at some later date: for a vacation, a hobby, long-term financial security, or retirement savings. If we then get something we need at a special price, we have to take the money from our savings account. We know that it will not be scary to 'invade' this special-purpose deposit with a particular goal, because we only have to scrimp for a little while—a few months. Savings goal achieved: hurrah! We now know that we can achieve our next financial goal, because we did it last time. And so we will be able to continue with another significant goal...

CHAPTER 6

Managing Debt

So, there's a lot of bad choices that we want to avoid. How do we build the good ones? Start with this strategy. Step 1: Always pay off your credit card debt. Always. No discussion. If you can't pay off the debt, you can't afford the purchase. You can't work on your financial picture until you've cleaned up this mess. Step 1.1: Only swipe the credit card if you already have the money in your checking account to cover the purchase. If you do these two things, your credit card debt problems will take care of themselves in perpetuity.

Step 2: Simplify life. Instead of worrying about ten credit card payments, invalid checks, budgeting to the dollar, etc., get yourself down to one simple budget unit. If you think budgeting is hard, remember Step 1: think simple. That means easy math so you can find some breathing room. Step 3: Make whatever ends meet. This includes selling stuff to keep the bank account "off the red". Minimalism affords simplicity, less stress, and adherence to the Rules of Engagement (of Step 1). Can't make the payment? Do you really need that car sitting in your driveway if it's mortgaging peace of mind for a family of five? No. Take 20 minutes and sell it. Buy a beater with what you wouldn't have spent on car insurance had you kept the LandYacht.

CHAPTER 7

Building Emergency Funds

When we consider the long-term need, it is not certain how much additional money you have for fundamental goals such as shopping or saving. Moreover, it confirms existing expectations in 2009 - a fund for the financing of emergency funds is necessary for individuals and families.

In late November 2008, the US Department of Commerce released updated statistics on consumer spending suggesting that, after increasing 1.1% last May, personal disposable income fell 0.2% in June, partly as a result of the first tax incentive check run in May, and personal consumption spending collected 0.2% in June. Initial consumption data show the continuation of the decline in the increase of product spending in the middle of 2008. These statistics show that while personal income is expected to stabilize in 2008 owing to the early 2008 crisis stimulus payments, disposable income is anticipated to rise further in 2009 as the impact of the economic slowdown on unemployment and monetary income declines.

In a recent release from Ally Bank in cooperation with USA Today, 89 percent of respondents feel that they have reduced or eliminated their savings priorities. In fact, the poll found that of those responding, 47 percent said that they have dropped their 401(k) contributions, 31 percent stopped contributing to other savings accounts, 22 percent used money from their emergency savings account, and 13 percent used money from their Roth IRA.

According to the National Foundation for Credit Counseling's annual financial literacy survey - 2013, to which 2,037 adults have been interviewed in March, 24% of those surveyed have little or no money for unexpected expenses, and 22% have the same issue when it comes to retirement savings. During this challenging period, if emergency funds have not been able to provide for a secure financial life, people have to follow special strategies.

Many Americans, ill-prepared to face the hard times brought on by the economic downturn, have now found that they face severe consequences. However, those Americans who had an emergency account in place have been able to survive this turbulent period without having to live on a deficit. Therefore, an emergency fund is a basic element for a healthy financial life.

CHAPTER 8

Protecting Your Assets

Remember to combine different types of protection so that if one of the legs buckles you still have a solid structure to support your vision and your family. This is called diversification. Using many different types of protection will also decrease the chance of something going wrong to all parts of your strategy at the same time. For those who have fledgling wealth, your most important type of asset protection is insurance. Unfortunately, there are as many different types of insurance as there are fellas who want to sell you insurance and similar to loan providers and debt products, some insurance types are true asset protectors, while others do nothing but feed you stress and fear. In the next wealth protection section, I make recommendations about the types of insurance you should consider.

Once you have built monetary wealth, it is important to protect your wealth and your assets. There are some common tactics that everyone should use to secure their assets, and there are some that are more customized to specific financial situations. There are a lot of things you can do to make sure that your assets are safe and that your family would be taken care of if something were to happen to you. Asset protection can also remove major stress from your life, stress which can negatively affect your physical health. Some things that you will read about in the Wealth Accumulation and Wealth Management Roadmaps could also be considered protection tactics. For example, setting up special accounts for different purposes can protect your wealth from the tax man, website savings accounts can make your household cash flow more predictable, building safer portfolios can protect you from extreme financial events and using insurance can protect your wealth from accidents, job loss or premature death.

CHAPTER 9

Building Multiple Streams of Income

Investors who want more should also discover the process of building wealth and security with the ultimate goal of achieving financial freedom or an early comfortable retirement, no matter where you stand financially. The advice includes how to find the appropriate long-term real wealth stocks, reinvesting in 70-90% stocks, and having other sources of income than your government-provided pension. The goal will be achieved with value growth by investing in companies and real estate properties.

With this concrete plan to achieve financial independence in just a matter of a few years on your road to financial freedom, you will learn how to master the required income-generating investments. Each chapter includes the necessary financial backstops to understand the long-term return on investment of investing in value companies or income-producing real estate. The content is easy to delve into for readers of all financial horizons. Even a novice with basic business knowledge will understand the importance of investing in lower-valued companies for their future financial success or the types of income-producing real estate that will help them achieve their investment goals.

We all dream of stopping trading our time for money one day. In order to reach this milestone, and unless you are planning to win the lottery or become the next superstar, you will have to create and develop multiple streams of income. One income is not enough, even with the help of your accumulated property, to secure the safety net you deserve during your golden age. And it is by investing in real estate and value companies that you will manage to develop these additional revenues.

CHAPTER 10

Real Estate Investment

Real estate Vs REITs: If you are not ready for the hustle of managing your vacant land, consider investing in real estate investment trusts. Real estate investment trusts (REITs) offer the benefit of real estate investing as well as an investment in a publicly traded company such as Ferrari, Bitcoin, or Apple on a stock exchange. Besides, it offers an excellent source of investment income. When investing in REITs, you own a portion of a real estate portfolio with various property types. The investor doesn't have the responsibility of managing the property, though they can suffer the risk and reward of people owning low occupation rates in their properties. There are two types, either equity REITs: which primarily earn rent, or mortgage REITs. The mortgage REITs are responsible for loaning money. It allows publicly traded companies to compete at the same level as a bank or government entity.

Real estate is a tangible investment, profitable for consistent rental income and long-term appreciation, which are the two wealthiest-building synergistic financial profit petcock. Real estate is a significant wealth-building vehicle for the investor who undertakes sophisticated property investment with due diligence and execution because it is straightforward to leverage and can be packed on an aggressive monthly cash return. Investing in real estate has two main ways of doing it, either physical asset or buying real estate investment trusts (REITs). Investing in rental property offers predictable income along with capital appreciation. It has significant tax advantages over other investment vehicles. Real estate investors tend to become reservoirs by being experts in the local markets and understanding lifestyle, economy, and jobs. This type of investor insulates oneself from economic downturns, as cash flow is more likely to remain secure than the dividend from stocks or the interest from bonds. If you are looking for certainty and to be a doer, real estate investment can lead you to financial freedom.

CHAPTER 11

Retirement Planning

An orderly, long-term playbook is available to build wealth and security. It is called the Financial Freedom Roadmap. It captures individual financial goals in a clear visual way and provides tactical details related to established milestones. How far you wish to go on the roadmap is unique to you. Your final destination will depend on your personal goals, comfort with investing, and the lifestyle you want to maintain before and during retirement, now and in the future. For most people, the goal is not necessarily to be completely financially independent right now, but to achieve a level of security now – like having money for an emergency – and work toward complete financial independence over a period of years. Financial independence is thus a more complex equation that depends on your total required spending and how much money you have accumulated to fund it over what could be a long period of time – also known as your drawdown period. For most people, plan realization would be an evolving process, and the peace of mind from having a plan in place can be quite extraordinary.

Most people desire financial security to some extent, and many aim to achieve financial independence and the freedom to pursue a variety of life goals. However, life is complex and busy, and many people may not pursue clearly defined financial strategies, not because they do not recognize the importance of financial security and independence but because they are not sure where to start. If you are reading this guide – or accessing this roadmap materialized through financial coaching or other learning mechanisms - you have likely taken the first step to helping yourself.

CHAPTER 12

Estate Planning

Estate planning is not only for the wealthy; families of all income levels can benefit from an estate plan. Estate planning is the process of building, preserving, and distributing the structure for the incremental steps of attaining your desired results and leaving behind a lasting impression of the life you lived and cared about your family members therein. Many estate planning tools can reduce or eliminate estate taxes, plan for unexpected illness or accidents, or even avoid probate. You want to make sure that your direct resources are utilized by competent individuals who may manage and create the estate plan, reduce taxes, conserve financial resources, or provide assistance when necessary while maintaining a degree of privacy. Following an established estate plan can also relieve potential family stress, estate tax, or arguments, thereby securing final goodbyes and a lasting legacy. It is important to involve family members who are beneficiaries in your estate plan and talk about payout with trusted heirs, according to the Trust or Will. To underscore the importance of estate planning in maintaining harmony among your beneficiaries, meet with your family members during the estate planning process as long-term familiarity could be helpful. If necessary, consider meeting with and sharing thoughts with other individuals, but avoid giving certain individuals preferences. Certain families may face estate taxes if they qualify as grandparents when establishing a 529 plan; the lifetime estate gift tax exclusion will be up to the equivalent of five years of gift taxes per year and will ensure an exclusion. Retitling real estate assets, establishing a QPRT, or funding irrevocable life insurance trusts could apply more funds in other years to provide for future expenses. So, it is a good strategy to remove appreciating assets from their estates, thereby also reducing potential taxes.

Why estate planning? You want to leave a financial legacy to your family members. You can also call their attention to the benefits of having a will or trust. Financial planning and involvement with an estate planning lawyer can help you take that first step towards leaving a legacy. Estate planning will involve additional professionals, such as an estate planning attorney, and possibly life insurance or other investment personnel.

CHAPTER 13

Tax Planning Strategies

Strategy #2: The Effective Tax Rate – Not the Marginal One Counts. Few people truly understand the tax code or the impact on their overall finances. Many people mistakenly believe that the marginal tax rates are more important than the effective tax rates. The effective tax rate is the total amount of tax as a percentage of taxable income. Let's illustrate the difference. The marginal tax rate is the exact percentage you will pay on the next dollar you earn. In the United States, it can range from as low as 0% to as high as 39.6%. The effective tax rate is a percentage that represents an individual's total tax liability as a proportion of their total income. This is the percentage of your taxable income. Most are surprised to learn that effective tax rates do not increase as quickly as marginal tax rates. In fact, there are times when individuals should be strategizing plans to create more income to reach the maximum of an effective tax rate.

One of the most complex subject matters in the financial industry is taxes. In this chapter, we will give you some strategies that you can employ to help legally reduce your taxes. Full chapter. Before we dive into the different tax-advantaged strategies that are available, we want to share three overarching tax planning strategies that are applicable across the board. Entrepreneur Magazine defined a tax strategy as one where the business owner has an "accumulation plan that calls for the discovery of income in virtually all areas of the business and the postponement, reduction and sometimes elimination of taxes wherever appropriate... We start by maximizing the benefits allowed by law and work backward from there..." Strategy #1: Tax Deferral S&P 500.

CHAPTER 14

Insurance Planning

Life is full of unexpected surprises and you may never know what will happen from one day to the next. Insurance plays an important part in protecting both your assets and your loved ones, in times of trouble. What is often not realized is the impact an unexpected event can have on your current lifestyle and future plans. Just as you have taken care to build your wealth over the years, protection should form part of your financial roadmap. In life, nothing is really certain except uncertainty and while we plan for the best, it is prudent to prepare for the worst as well. Emerging trends over the past decade have been unprecedented natural calamities, like floods, certain risks involved with exchange-traded funds and uncertainty inherent with investments. Personal risks are events in an individual's life that may lead to suffering a financial loss. Its effects will be keenly felt if it were to occur, e.g. an unexpected medical bill, premature death or disability. People insure their various risks by paying relatively small amounts of money regularly to create a risk pool.

Insurance provides protection from the financial consequences of dying or becoming disabled. While protecting the family against the potential negative financial consequences of dying or dying too soon is a crucial part of the protection plan, a financial planner should also be concerned with what happens if the main provider just becomes disabled or cannot earn an income. Insurance planning includes providing protection from the big 'ifs', or cover for loss of income due to temporary or permanent disability. Other types of insurance you may consider include the short-term variety, such as covering the car, contents, and the family's health. As part of your comprehensive financial plan, an evaluation might be necessary to determine if the benefits offered by your employer are sufficient or if additional cover is required.

CHAPTER 15

Building a Support System

Once you have a support system established, have regular get-togethers where you discuss your progress. Working with partners on a monthly, semi-annual, or whenever basis allows you to see how you compare with your peers and what you can learn from their experiences. Share your mistakes as well as your successes. If you need help, ask for guidance. Why should you reinvent the wheel when you can learn from others? Surround yourself with better role models and you will be inspired.

Finding a good support system can be crucial when you are working towards long-term goals. If your immediate family is not supportive, look for friends, co-workers, or other people who are aiming for similar goals. If you wish to move up the "ladder of success" or purchase income-generating properties, you probably want to meet and network with people who are already living that life. Attend workshops and meet-up groups concerning your area of interest and become familiar with an expert or two. Look for people who are positive and your life will be enriched. If your current associates are negative and cynical on the subject, you may wish to explore their motivations and attitudes.

CHAPTER 16

Taking Action and Staying Motivated

The process starts with clarifying your goals. Only then is it time to find out where you are today. As often as every six months, assess your progress and make any changes that are needed. It's worth the time. Financial freedom is less about life doing what you want without financial roadblocks, but rather more about having the resources when you need them. It happens by taking steps to educate yourself, to act early, and to make changes when it makes sense rather than when it becomes urgent. Building and maintaining financial security will help minimize the stress typical in emergency situations. The positive impact this has on life is immense. Success doesn't necessarily mean you want to accumulate and maintain a seven-figure bank account. Depending on your goals, security could be established with a few hundred thousand dollars. According to your individual circumstances, the path is flexible. You have reached financial freedom when you have the resources to help make things work according to your expectations, when you have choices along the way. What's helpful to commit now will likely be more beneficial sooner rather than later.

It's not enough to learn about the steps for moving toward financial freedom. Knowing what the steps are, but not doing anything about them, won't improve your financial situation. You must translate understanding what to do into action. The secret is to start wherever you are. It's easy to procrastinate when you think about all that you want to accomplish. This book outlines a simple financial planning process. There's no need to do more planning than can be practically used. These are very achievable steps to make a real difference. Even small improvements translate into substantial dollars over time. Use what's helpful and go at a pace that works well for you. An important part of getting value is to continue. Once you get going, it's easier to maintain momentum. With practice, taking these steps will become a habit that translates into lasting improvements to your life.